Revenge of the Lunch Ladies

The Hilarious Book of School Poetry

Kenn Nesbitt

m Meadowbrook Press
Distributed by Simon & Schuster
New York

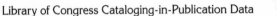

Library of Congress Cataloging-in-Publication Data

Nesbitt, Kenn.
  Revenge of the lunch ladies : the hilarious book of school poetry / by Kenn Nesbitt ;
illustrated by Mike and Carl Gordon.
      p. cm.
  Summary: "A collection of poems about the humorous ups and downs of school"
—Provided by publisher.
  Includes index.
  ISBN 0-88166-527-4 (Meadowbrook Press) ISBN 1-4169-4364-1 (Simon & Schuster)
  1. Elementary schools—Juvenile poetry. I. Gordon, Mike, ill. II. Gordon,
Carl, ill. III. Title.
PS3614.E47R48 2007
811'.54--dc22
                            2006103014

Project Director: Bruce Lansky
Coordinating Editor and Copyeditor: Angela Wiechmann
Editorial Assistant and Proofreader: Alicia Ester
Production Manager: Paul Woods
Graphic Design Manager: Tamara Peterson
Illustrations and Cover Art: Mike and Carl Gordon
Sketch Artist: Jeff Felson

Published by Meadowbrook Press, 5451 Smetana Drive, Minnetonka, Minnesota 55343

www.meadowbrookpress.com

BOOK TRADE DISTRIBUTION by Simon and Schuster, a division of Simon and Schuster, Inc.,
1230 Avenue of the Americas, New York, New York 10020

12 11 10 09 08 07   10 9 8 7 6 5 4 3 2 1

Printed in the United States of America

Dedication

For Isabella and Cooper

Acknowledgments

My thanks go out to all the kids who took the time to read and rate my poems in school and on Poetry4Kids.com and GigglePoetry.com. Your ratings helped decide which poems made it into this book and which did not. To Ann, Max, and Madison, thank you for giving me the time to write and for putting up with my insane travel schedule. I love you all. To Bruce, Angie, and the gang at Meadowbrook, a poet couldn't ask for a better team of editors. Thank you for helping make this book as good as it is. To High Overlord Zepton of Gleepax, thank you for the rescue shuttle and the use of the time disruptor, without which this book would not have been possible. And a big thank you to teachers, librarians, administrators, and lunch ladies everywhere for making school fun for your young readers.

Many thanks to the following teachers and their students
who tested poems for this collection:

Mark Benthall ....Lakeway Elementary ....Austin, TX
Sara Burgwinkle ....McCarthy Elementary...................Framingham, MA
Connie Cooper....................Lincoln Elementary......................Fairbault, MN
Cindy Crayder.....................Whitemarsh Elementary School ....Lafayette Hill, PA
Pat Dodds...........................Robinson Elementary School.........Fresno, CA
Shana Duffine......................Whitemarsh Elementary School ....Lafayette Hill, PA
Kathy Kenney-Marshall .....McCarthy Elementary...................Framingham, MA
Simie Krieger......................Whitemarsh Elementary School ....Lafayette Hill, PA
Julie Lambert..Erlanger, KY
Carolyn Larsen...................Rum River Elementary..................Andover, MN
Linda Lineman ....District-Topton Elementary...........Topton, PA
Erin McKelvey.....................Whitemarsh Elementary School ....Lafayette Hill, PA
Maren Morgan-Thomson...District-Topton Elementary...........Topton, PA
Chad Murray.......................Whitemarsh Elementary School ....Lafayette Hill, PA
Jenny Myer ....East Elementary ....New Richmond, WI
Sarah Nutt..........................Lake City Public Schools ....Lake City, MN
Toby Salmon ....Whitemarsh Elementary School ....Lafayette Hill, PA
Margie Stein.......................Whitemarsh Elementary School ....Lafayette Hill, PA
Suzanne Storbeck ....Holy Name School........................Wayzata, MN
Kathi Young........................Whitemarsh Elementary School ....Lafayette Hill, PA

Contents

Welcome Back to School

"Dear students, the summer has ended.
The school year at last has begun.
But this year is totally different.
I promise we'll only have fun.

"We won't study any mathematics,
and recess will last all day long.
Instead of the Pledge of Allegiance,
we'll belt out a rock 'n' roll song.

"We'll only play games in the classroom.
You're welcome to bring in your toys.
It's okay to run in the hallways.
It's great if you make lots of noise.

"For homework, you'll play your Nintendo.
You'll have to watch lots of TV.
For field trips we'll go to the movies
and get lots of candy for free.

"The lunchroom will only serve chocolate
and Triple-Fudge Sundaes Supreme."
Yes, that's what I heard from my teacher
before I woke up from my dream.

School Supplies

Backpack.
Fruit snack.
Water bottle, too.
Calculator.
French translator.
Pink eraser.
Glue.

Notebooks.
Workbooks.
Poster paper.
Pens.
Dictionary.
Stationery.
Presents for my
    friends.

Lunchbox.
Tube socks.
Watercolors.
Tape.
Yellow pencils.
Plastic stencils—
one for every shape.

Wristwatch.
Stopwatch.
Cell phone.
DVD.
New computer.
Motor scooter.
Giant-screen TV.

That's my
list of
all I
need to buy.
I never knew a
shopping list could
make my mother cry.

My Dream of School Supplies

I had a dream of school supplies,
where paper clips could talk,
where poster paper hung around
with marking pens and chalk.

The stationery idled
while the pencils madly raced.
The clocks went 'round in circles,
and the glue sticks merely paced.

The binders were inseparable.
They bonded with the tape.
The workbooks exercised and helped
the stencils stay in shape.

Some calculators added
to the numbers in this land,
and music was provided by
a singing rubber band.

These things were weird and kind of cool,
but *this* was even cooler:
The dictionaries all looked up
to me—I was the ruler.

My New School

You won't believe the crazy things
I'm learning how to do.
I'm learning how to juggle,
ride a unicycle, too.

I now know how to twist balloons
in many different shapes
and how to make a costume
out of multicolored drapes.

I've learned to run in floppy shoes
and how to dye my hair.
I've even learned the graceful art
of dancing with a bear.

For when we moved, my parents looked
at many different towns,
but chose a place with just one school:
a school for circus clowns.

Robots in the School

We had never seen a robot
till they commandeered our school.
They arrived here from the future
when they needed to refuel.

They invaded every classroom.
They came clanking through the halls.
If you looked inside the bathrooms,
you'd see robots in the stalls.

They surrounded all the teachers
and propelled them out the door.
Then they headed for the offices
in search of even more.

They ejected the custodian
and principal as well,
plus the secretary, nurse,
and all the other personnel.

They intruded in the lunchroom
and evicted all the cooks.
They expelled our good librarian
and plundered all her books.

Then they came across a small surprise
in section eight-one-one—
just a book of goofy poetry
that looked like lots of fun.

When they opened it and read
about some silly school supplies,
their antennae started sparking
as they snickered in surprise.

Then a poem that they read
about the students' favorite sports
made them giggle uncontrollably
with belly laughs and snorts.

When they read about the principal
that nobody could find,
all their heads began to rattle,
and their gears began to grind.

Then they read a final poem,
and their circuits overloaded.
They guffawed so hard they couldn't stop,
and all their heads exploded.

Now the school is back to normal.
All the teachers have returned,
and we're happy for the all-important
lesson that we learned:

If the robots ever come again,
they're in for loads of pain,
since we found out funny poetry
can melt a robot's brain.

Let Me Out of the Classroom

(sing to the tune of "Take Me Out to the Ball Game")

Let me out of the classroom.
Let me out of the school.
I'm not so good at geography.
I would rather be watching TV.
It's still twenty minutes till recess,
and lunch is hours away.
Someone please, please, please let me out
of the class today!

Someone's here with a note now.
Teacher's calling my name.
He says my mother is right outside.
I should go, and she'll give me a ride
to my yearly dentist appointment.
Oh, I forgot it's today!
Teacher, please, please, please
   help me out!
Won't you let me stay?

Home for the Day
(sing to the tune of "Home on the Range")

Oh, give me the phone,
so that I can call home,
and my mom can come get me today.
I'm feeling so sick.
Get me out of here quick.
Oh, I wish Mom would take me away.

Home, home for the day.
How I wish Mom would take me away.
For the truth of it is,
teacher gave us a quiz,
and I just wasn't ready today.

11

All My Great Excuses

I started on my homework,
but my pen ran out of ink…
My hamster ate my homework…
My computer's on the blink…

I tripped and dropped my homework
in the soup my mom was cooking…
My brother flushed it down the toilet
when I wasn't looking…

My mother ran my homework
through the washer and the dryer…
An airplane crashed into our house…
My homework caught on fire…

Tornadoes blew my notes away...
Volcanoes rocked our town...
My books were taken hostage
by an evil killer clown...

Some aliens abducted me...
I had a shark attack...
A pirate swiped my homework
and refused to give it back...

I worked on these excuses
so darned long my teacher said,
"I think you'll find it's easier
to do the work instead."

My Teacher Calls Me "Sweetie Cakes"

My teacher calls me "sweetie cakes."
My classmates think it's funny
to hear her call me "angel face"
or "pookie bear" or "honey."

She calls me "precious baby doll."
She calls me "pumpkin pie"
or "doodlebug" or "honey bunch"
or "darling butterfly."

This class is so embarrassing,
I need to find another—
just any class at all
in which the teacher's not my mother.

My Lunch

A candy bar.
A piece of cake.
A lollipop.
A chocolate shake.
A jelly donut.
Chocolate chips.
Some gummi worms
and licorice whips.

A candy cane.
A lemon drop.
Some bubblegum
and soda pop.
Vanilla wafers.
Cherry punch.
(My mom slept in
while I made lunch.)

Revenge of the Lunch Ladies

(sing to the tune of "Animal Fair")

I went to the lunchroom, and there,
last week on a double dare,
I said the meat was too gross to eat
and smelled like my underwear.
I shouldn't have been rude
by making such fun of the food,
for though they were riled,
   the lunch ladies smiled,
and said I had started a feud.

Today when I went there to eat,
they served up some monkey meat.
I ran out quick when I nearly got sick,
but then I went back to my seat.
The lunchroom ladies sighed
to see that I practically cried,
then served up a hunk of
   barbecued skunk,
and that was the reason I died.
I died! I died! I died!

Swinging from the Lights

We're swinging from the lights.
We're standing on our chairs.
We're bouncing off the walls.
We're sliding down the stairs.
We're running in the halls.
We're slamming all the doors.
We're jumping off our desks.
We're skidding on the floors.
We'd rather use the swings.
We'd rather use the slide.
Too bad! Today it's raining,
so recess is inside.

My Teacher Ate My Homework

My teacher ate my homework,
which I thought was rather odd.
He sniffed at it and smiled
with an approving sort of nod.

He took a little nibble—
it's unusual, but true—
then had a somewhat larger bite
and gave a thoughtful chew.

I think he must have liked it,
for he really went to town.
He gobbled it with gusto,
and he wolfed the whole thing down.

He licked off all his fingers,
gave a burp, and said, "You pass."
I guess that's how they grade you
when you're in a cooking class.

I Have Noodles in My Nostrils

I have noodles in my nostrils.
I have noodles on my nose.
There are noodles on my cheeks and chin
and dripping down my clothes.

I've got more upon my forehead.
Some are sticking to my neck.
It's completely disconcerting.
I'm a noodle-covered wreck.

I can see them on my kneecaps,
and I know they're in my shoes.
(When I stand, they're somewhat squishy,
and I feel them start to ooze.)

There are several in my pockets.
There's a handful in my hair.
And I'm pretty sure that some are even
in my underwear.

So try not to do what I did:
I'm a total nincompoop,
and I fell asleep at lunch
while eating chicken noodle soup.

My Teacher Took My iPod

My teacher took my iPod.
She said they had a rule:
I couldn't bring it into class
or even to the school.

She said she would return it;
I'd have it back that day.
But then she tried my headphones on
and gave a click on "Play."

She looked a little startled,
but after just awhile,
she made sure we were occupied
and cracked a wicked smile.

Her body started swaying.
Her toes began to tap.
She started grooving in her seat
and rocking to the rap.

My teacher said she changed her mind.
She thinks it's now okay
to bring my iPod into class.
She takes it every day.

What I Told Mrs. Morris When She Asked How I Was Feeling Today

"Grumbly, grouchy,
groggy, grumpy,
sleepy, slouchy,
fussy, frumpy,
whiny, weary,
cranky, crazy,
dingy, dreary,
loopy, lazy,
dizzy, drowsy,
crusty, crummy,
loony, lousy,
scruffy, scummy,
bleary, batty,
shaky, shabby,
rusty, ratty,
cruddy, crabby.
That describes it,
Mrs. Morris.
Thank you for the
new thesaurus."

State Capitals

Our homework assignment was simply to write down
the capitals for every state.
I wrote down MONTANA, NEW YORK, INDIANA.
I thought I was doing just great.

I wrote down ALASKA, WYOMING, NEBRASKA,
VIRGINIA, VERMONT, SOUTH DAKOTA.
I also wrote MARYLAND, UTAH, RHODE ISLAND,
CONNECTICUT, MAINE, MINNESOTA.

I wrote down all fifty, and just to make certain,
I checked them and then *double*-checked them.
I handed them in with the rest of the class
for the teacher to go and correct them.

I guess I must not have been paying attention,
or maybe I'm just a bit deaf.
Whatever the reason, I misunderstood,
and so I got a capital F.

Basketball's My Favorite Sport

Basketball's my favorite sport.
I dribble up and down the court.
The ball goes bouncing off my toes
and beans the teacher on the nose.

He stumbles back and grabs his nose
and hits the wall and down he goes.
The other players stop and stare.
They've never heard the teacher swear.

With no one playing anymore,
I grab the ball. I shoot. I score.
I love this game! It's so much fun.
The teacher cried, but, hey—we won!

VISITORS HOME

10 12

Class Gas

The teacher passed out and fell right off her chair.
My classmates are crying and gasping for air.
The hamster is howling and hiding his head.
The plants by the window are practically dead.

There's gas in the class; it's completely my fault.
It smells like a chemical-weapons assault.
So try to remember this lesson from me:
Don't take off your shoes in class after PE.

Today I Had a Rotten Day

Today I had a rotten day
as I was coming in from play.
I accidentally stubbed my toes
and tripped and fell and whacked my nose.
I chipped a tooth. I cut my lip.
I scraped my knee. I hurt my hip.
I pulled my shoulder, tweaked my ear,
and got a bruise upon my rear.

I banged my elbow, barked my shin.
A welt is forming on my chin.
My pencil poked me in the thigh.
I got an eyelash in my eye.
I sprained my back. I wrenched my neck.
I'm feeling like a total wreck.
So that's the last time I refuse
when teacher says to tie my shoes.

28

You Can Argue with a Tennis Ball

You can argue with a tennis ball
or argue with your hat.
You can argue with bananas
or a broken baseball bat.

You can argue with your locker.
You can argue with your shoe.
You can argue all day long
until your face is turning blue.

You can argue with a pickle.
You can argue with a bee.
It's a fact that you can argue
with most anything you see.

You can argue with the football field
or argue with the bleachers.
But I've found it isn't very smart
to argue with the teachers.

Perfect

Today I managed something
that I've never done before:
I turned in this week's spelling quiz
and got a perfect score.

Although my score was perfect,
it appears I'm not too bright.
I got a perfect zero—
not a single answer right.

At History, I'm Hopeless

At history, I'm hopeless.
At spelling, I stink.
In music, I'm useless.
From science, I shrink.
At art, I'm atrocious.
In sports, I'm a klutz.
At reading, I'm rotten.
And math makes me nuts.
At language, I'm lousy.
Computers? I'm cursed.
In drama, I'm dreadful.
My writing's the worst.
There's only one subject
I'm sure I would pass,
but they don't teach
video games in my class.

Peter Passed a Note Today

Peter passed a note today.
He gave the note to Anna.
She opened it and read it,
then she handed it to Hannah.

The note made Hannah giggle
so she passed it on to Cody,
who read it with a smile before
he slid the note to Brody.

Then Brody read the contents,
and he gave it to Luann,
who opened it and chuckled
and directed it to Dan.

He read it with a snicker,
then he tossed the note to Jon,
who couldn't help but chortle
as he passed it on to Sean.

The teacher heard us laughing,
and she saw what Sean was holding.
She walked across the room
and took the note he was unfolding.

We thought we'd get in trouble,
but she gave it back to Sean
and smiled because it read,
"The teacher's awesome. Pass it on."

Science Homework

I hope that you believe me,
for I wouldn't tell a lie.
I cannot turn my science homework in
and this is why:

I messed up the assignment
that you gave us yesterday.
It burbled from its test tube
and went slithering away.

It wriggled off the table,
and it landed with a splat,
convulsed across my bedroom floor
and terrorized the cat.

It shambled down the staircase
with a horrid glorping noise.
It wobbled to the family room
and gobbled all my toys.

It tumbled to the kitchen
and digested every plate.
That slimy blob enlarged
with every item that it ate.

It writhed around the living room
digesting lamps and chairs,
then snuck up on our napping dog
and caught him unawares.

I came to school upset today.
My head's in such a fog.
But this is my excuse:
You see, my homework ate my dog.

My Family Thinks I'm Crazy

My family thinks I'm crazy—
that I'm loopy as a loon.
They're certain that the funny farm
is coming for me soon.

They say I'm certifiable.
They claim that I'm deranged.
They tell me that I really ought
to have my head exchanged.

They're utterly befuddled,
which I think is pretty cool.
It drives my family crazy
that I'm crazy for my school.

Oh My Darling, Valentine

(sing to the tune of "Clementine")

In a toy store
on a Sunday
with a dollar forty-nine,
I need something,
just a dumb thing,
for my brand-new
valentine.

Oh my darling,
oh my darling,
oh my darling,
valentine.
I'm uneasy,
kind of queasy,
but you're still my
valentine.

Yes, it happened
in the classroom
when you said,
"Will you be mine?"
I was muddled
and befuddled,
so I answered,
"Yeah, that's fine."

Then you called me
in the lunchroom.
You had saved a
place in line.
And I knew that
it was true that
I was now your
valentine.

I went shopping
for a present,
and I saw this
blinking sign:
"Here's a pleasant
little present
for a brand-new
valentine."

So I bought it,
and I brought it
in my backpack
right at nine.
Do you like it?
It's a spy kit
with a flashlight
you can shine.

I could tell you
didn't like it
when you said I
was a swine.
How exciting!
I'm delighting.
I have no more
valentine.

Till another
person stopped me,
and she asked,
"Will you be mine?"
This is crushing!
Oh, I'm blushing.
I've another
valentine.

39

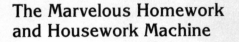

The Marvelous Homework and Housework Machine

Attention all students! Attention all kids!
Hold onto your horses! Hold onto your lids!
We have just exactly the thing that you need
whenever you've way too much homework to read.

The Marvelous Homework and Housework Machine
will always make sure that your bedroom is clean.
It loves to write book reports ten pages long,
then put all your toys away where they belong.

This wonderful gadget will do all your math,
then mop up your messes and go take your bath.
The Marvelous Homework and Housework Machine
is truly like no other gizmo you've seen.

It hangs up your clothes on their hangers and hooks,
then reads all your boring geography books.
It brings you a pillow to give you a rest,
then brushes your teeth and prepares for your test.

This thing is amazing—I'm sure you'll agree.
It feeds you dessert while you're watching TV.
There's only one thing this device will not do:
It won't eat your Brussels sprouts—they're, like, PU!

Hannah's Hammer

Hannah has a hammer
that she keeps beside her bed.
It's shinier than silver,
and it's heavier than lead.

She wakes to her alarm each day—
it's time to go to school.
And Hannah has the perfect way
to utilize her tool.

And as she leaves the house for school
her mother stares in shock.
Yes, every day her mother
has to buy a brand-new clock.

I'm Staying Home from School Today

I'm staying home from school today.
I'd rather be in bed,
pretending that I have a pain
that's pounding in my head.

I'll say I have a stomachache.
I'll claim I've got the flu.
I'll shiver like I'm cold
and hold my breath until I'm blue.

I'll fake a cough. I'll fake a sneeze.
I'll say my throat is sore.
If necessary, I can throw
a tantrum on the floor.

I'm sure I'll get away with it.
Of that, there's little doubt.
But even so, I really hope
my students don't find out.

43

44

Teacher, Teacher, How's My Singing?

(sing to the tune of "The Battle Hymn of the Republic")

Oh, I had to write a poem 'cause my teacher said I should,
but the poems that I tried to write weren't coming out so good,
and I figured everything I wrote would be misunderstood.
Instead, I wrote this song.

Chorus
Teacher, teacher, how's my singing?
Is it painful? Is it stinging?
Have your eardrums started ringing?
I hope you like my song!

Yes, I had to write a poem, but I couldn't get it right,
though I sharpened all my pencils, and I stayed up half the night.
So I grabbed my dictionary, and I chucked it out of sight,
and then I wrote this song.

Chorus

I Have to Write a Poem

I have to write a poem,
but I really don't know how.
So maybe I'll just make a rhyme
with something dumb, like *cow*.

Okay, I'll write about a cow,
but that's so commonplace.
I think I'll have to make her be…
a cow from outer space!

My cow will need a helmet
and a space suit and a ship.
Of course, she'll keep a blaster
in the holster on her hip.

She'll hurtle through the galaxy
on meteoric flights
to battle monkey aliens
in huge karate fights.

She'll duel with laser sabers
while avoiding lava spray
to vanquish evil emperors
and always save the day.

I hope the teacher likes my tale:
"Amazing Astro Cow."
Yes, that's the poem I will write
as soon as I learn how.

My Excellent Education

How to juggle.
How to hop.
How to make
my knuckles pop.
How to whinny.
How to cluck.
How to talk
like Donald Duck.
How to wiggle
both my ears.
How to fake
convincing tears.

How to yo-yo.
Capture flies.
Roll my tongue
and cross my eyes.
How to make a
piggy snout.
How to make
my eyes bug out.
These are things
I learned in school.
Education—
ain't it cool?

The Principal Is Missing

The principal is missing.
He's nowhere to be found.
The teachers tried to page him,
and they've hunted all around.

He isn't in the staff room.
He isn't in the gym,
and all the kids are wondering
just what's become of him.

We've looked in every classroom.
We've peeked in every hall.
We even checked the bathrooms
and inspected every stall.

He isn't in his closet.
He's not behind his door.
He isn't underneath his desk
or hiding in a drawer.

If you should see our principal,
please send him back to school,
and tell him we apologize.
We know that we were cruel.

Please tell him that we miss him.
We're sorry we were mean.
But tell him next Saint Patrick's Day
he needs to wear some green.

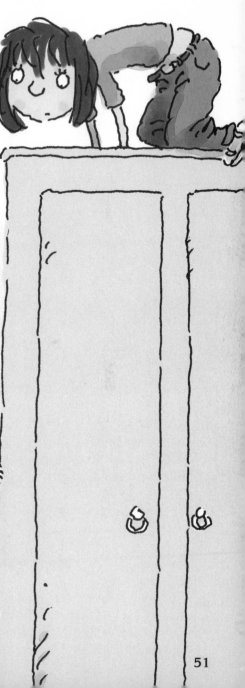

Our Teacher's a Football Fanatic

Our teacher's a football fanatic.
It's all that he has on his mind.
He listens to games on his headphones
and frets when his team is behind.

He jumps up and down when they're winning.
He screams when they fumble a pass.
We know we're supposed to be reading,
but watching him's simply a gas.

Our principal walked in on Friday,
and he was too angry to speak.
Our substitute started on Monday.
Our teacher's been benched for a week.

If School Were More Like Baseball

If school were more like baseball,
we'd always get to play.
We'd hang out in the sunshine
and run around all day.

We wouldn't have to study.
We'd practice and we'd train.
And best of all, they'd cancel
whenever there was rain.

My Girlfriend

I now have a girlfriend, though I don't like girls.
I haven't much money, but I buy her pearls.
I'm always embarrassed, but I give her flowers
and talk on the phone every evening for hours.
We go to the movies, and she gets to pick.
She likes holding hands, though it makes me feel sick.
She likes when I smell good, so I take a bath.
I do what she asks me, and she does my math.

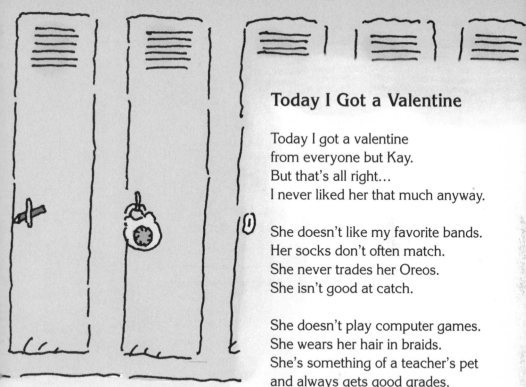

Today I Got a Valentine

Today I got a valentine
from everyone but Kay.
But that's all right…
I never liked her that much anyway.

She doesn't like my favorite bands.
Her socks don't often match.
She never trades her Oreos.
She isn't good at catch.

She doesn't play computer games.
She wears her hair in braids.
She's something of a teacher's pet
and always gets good grades.

She dots her *i*'s with little hearts.
She's always reading books.
Whenever I'm around, she gives me
such confusing looks.

But oh my goodness,
 here comes Kay—
and what is this I see?
It seems she has an extra special
valentine for me.

It's big and red and has the words,
"Will you be mine today?"
I've always said there's no one else
I like as much as Kay!

55

What to Do with a Dinosaur

This morning a dinosaur tromped into school,
ferocious, atrocious, and dripping with drool.

He had to be practically twenty feet tall.
He banged around, looking for something to maul.

He stomped and he snorted; he bellowed and roared.
His head hit the ceiling and busted a board.

That beast was undoubtedly ready for lunch.
He snatched up a chair in his teeth with a *crunch*.

He stopped for a moment and thoughtfully chewed;
it seems he had smelled cafeteria food.

He spit out the chair and then plowed down the hall,
his tail swinging wildly and smashing the wall.

He burst through the doors of the lunchroom to see
the lunch ladies cling to their hairnets and flee.

He found the lasagna and gobbled it up,
then lapped up the lemonade, cup after cup.

He ransacked the salad bar, plundered dessert,
then stiffened and yelped as if suddenly hurt.

He let out a howl as he clutched at his side,
then gave out a gasp and fell over and died.

So next time a dinosaur comes to your school,
I think you'd do well to remember this rule:

Get out of the way of his bad attitude,
and make sure he eats cafeteria food.

I've Been Surfing Lots of Websites

(sing to the tune of "I've Been Working on the Railroad")

I've been surfing lots of websites
here at school all day.
Now I'm getting all these pop-ups,
and they will not go away.
This computer has a virus.
Spyware is using all the RAM.
Every time I check my e-mail,
all I get is spam.

Pop-ups left and right.
Spam all day and night.
Trojan horses on the hard drive, too.
Viruses and worms.
Cybernetic germs.
Don't know what I'm gonna do.

Hackers got my password in China.
Spammers got my address in Idaho-o.
Now I'm getting spyware from Thailand,
viruses from Mexico.

I'm freaking.
See the DVD drive groan.
See the memory go slow, slow, slow, slow.
See the monitor top smoke.
This computer's gonna blow!

When Sarah Surfs the Internet

When Sarah surfs the Internet,
she starts by checking mail.
She answers all her messages
from friends in great detail.

She plays a game—or maybe two—
and watches a cartoon,
then chats with kids in places
like Rwanda and Rangoon.

She reads about her favorite bands.
She buys an MP3.
She downloads movie trailers,
and she looks for stuff that's free.

She reads about celebrities
and dreams of wealth and fame,
then watches music videos,
and plays another game.

If you should say, "Your time is up.
I need to use the Net,"
she always whines, "I haven't got
my homework finished yet!"

Imaginary Friend

I came to school today
with my imaginary friend.
When everyone said hi to her,
I said, "She's just pretend."

But no one seemed to notice,
which I thought was pretty weird.
It turns out she'd imagined *me*,
so *poof!* I disappeared.

61

He Flies Down the Hall

(sing to the tune of "The Man on the Flying Trapeze")

Oh, he flies down the hall
with the greatest of ease—
the boy with the helmet
and pads on his knees.
The teachers give chase
as he panics and flees,
but his skateboard is taken away.

So he zips through the hall
on his scooter so fast,
his classmates all giggle
to see him sail past.
For thirty-eight seconds
he's having a blast,
then his scooter is taken away.

So he runs down the hall
with a whoop and a shout.
The kids can't believe
all the rules that he'll flout.
The principal nabs him:
"It's three strikes, you're out!"
Now he sits in detention today.

My Penmanship Is Pretty Bad

My penmanship is pretty bad.
My printing's plainly awful.
In truth, my writing looks so sad,
it ought to be unlawful.

I try, but still, I must confess
my writing looks like scribbles.
My pencil makes a painful mess.
My ballpoint leaks and dribbles.

My letters take up so much space,
they nearly can't be read.
The ones that should be lowercase
are capitals instead.

My p's and q's and r's and b's
are backward half the time.
When letters look as bad as these,
it's probably a crime.

My cursive's utter lack of style
will make you want to curse.
But even so, I have to smile—
my teacher's writing's worse.

Bed Head

I can't do a thing with my hairdo.
I've tried, but it's simply no use.
I can't make it stay where I put it today
with styling gel, hair spray, or mousse.

No bobby pin, brush, or bandanna
can get my hair under control.
I've tried every comb, every clip in my home
and covered my head with a bowl.

I've tried using forks in frustration.
I've tried using pokers and picks.
I've tried using straps; I've tried headbands and caps.
I've even tried shoestrings and sticks.

Regardless of how I attack it,
I simply cannot make it stay.
I guess I can't win, so I'll have to give in
and look like my students today.

April Fools' Day

Mackenzie put a whoopee cushion
on the teacher's chair.
Makayla told the teacher
that a bug was in her hair.

Alyssa brought an apple
with a purple gummi worm
and gave it to the teacher
just to see if she would squirm.

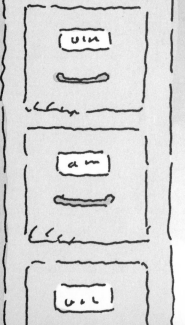

Elijah left a piece of plastic
dog-doo on the floor,
and Vincent put some plastic vomit
in the teacher's drawer.

Amanda put a goldfish
in the teacher's drinking glass.
These April Fools' Day pranks
are ones that *you* could try in class.

Before you go and use them, though,
there's something I should mention:
The teacher wasn't fooling
when she put us in detention.

The Teachers Jumped Out of the Windows

The teachers jumped out of the windows.
The principal ran for the door.
The nurse and librarian bolted.
They're not coming back anymore.

The counselor, hollering madly,
escaped out the door of the gym.
The coach and custodian shouted
and ran out the door after him.

The lunch ladies threw up their ladles,
then fled from the kitchen in haste,
and all of the students looked puzzled
as staff members scurried and raced.

We'd never seen anything like it.
But still, it was pretty darned cool
to see all the staff so excited
to leave on the last day of school.

71

Index

A

B

C

H

I

L

M

Also from Meadowbrook Press

When the Teacher Isn't Looking
Students and teachers will roar as Kenn Nesbitt pokes fun at silly school topics with dozens of wacky poems. With topics such as burping the ABCs and food fights, these poems cover everything that goes on while the teacher isn't looking. The rhymes in this book have earned A's when tested on kids—and are sure to make teachers smile as well.

Santa Got Stuck in the Chimney
This book contains 20 delightful poems full of Christmas cheer. Nesbitt's and Knaus's poems capture all the funny things that happen during the Christmas season—including hunting for a mall parking spot on the day after Thanksgiving, writing a list of the presents Santa forgot to bring, and eating unusual foods at a potluck Christmas dinner.

The Aliens Have Landed at Our School!
Children will love the imaginative world of Kenn Nesbitt, a world with mashed potatoes on the ceiling, skunks falling in love, antigravity machines, and aliens invading the school—all wonderfully brought to life in illustrations by Margeaux Lucas.

If Kids Ruled the School
Guaranteed to make you giggle, grin, and guffaw, this anthology is brimming with side-splitting poetry from Bruce Lansky, Kenn Nesbitt, and others. It touches on subjects like homework, tests and grades, show-and-tell, falling asleep in class, school lunches, awkward moments, bad hair, and the ups and downs experienced by every student in school.

No More Homework! No More Tests!
A hilarious collection of poems about school by the most popular children's poets, including Shel Silverstein, Jack Prelutsky, Bruce Lansky, Kenn Nesbitt, David L. Harrison, Colin McNaughton, Kalli Dakos, and others who know how to find humor in any subject.

My Teacher's in Detention
These 45 hilarious poems about school cover everything from homework and tests to detention and digesting school lunches. Well-known poets Bruce Lansky, Jack Prelutsky, and Kenn Nesbitt—plus many more great "giggle poets"—wrote these gems.

Kids Pick the Funniest Poems
Three hundred elementary-school kids will tell you that this book contains the funniest poems for kids—because they picked them! Not surprisingly, they chose many of the funniest poems ever written by favorites like Shel Silverstein, Jack Prelutsky, Jeff Moss, Judith Viorst, Bruce Lansky, and Kenn Nesbitt (plus poems by lesser-known writers that are just as funny). This book is guaranteed to please children ages 6–12!